Rocks and Soil

Jen Green

WAYLAND

First published in 2007 by Wayland
Copyright © Wayland 2007

Wayland
338 Euston Road
London NW1 3BH

Wayland Australia
Level 17/207 Kent Street
Sydney NSW 2000

Produced by Tall Tree Ltd
Editor: Jon Richards
Designer: Ben Ruocco
Consultant: John Williams

British Library Cataloguing in Publication
Data
 Green, Jen
   Rocks & soil. – (Our Earth)
   1. Rocks – Juvenile literature 2. Soils –
   Juvenile
   literature
   I. Title
   552

   ISBN-13: 9780750250061

Printed in China
Wayland is a division of Hachette
Children's Books.

Picture credits:
Cover Dreamstime.com/Stuart Elflett,
1 Dreamstime.com, 4 Dreamstime.com/
Rebecca Abell, 5 Dreamstime.com/Eric Foltz,
6 Digital Vision, 7t Dreamstime.com/Andy
Butler, 7m Dreamstime.com,
7b Dreamstime.com, 8 Dreamstime.com,
9 Dreamstime.com/Stuart Elflett,
10 Dreamstime.com/Ricardo Garza,
11 Dreamstime.com/N. Joy Neish,
12 Dreamstime.com/Scott Rothstein,
13 Dreamstime.com/Alexander Maksimov,
14 Dreamstime.com/Mark Bond,
15 Corbis/Didier Dutheil/Sygma, 16 Digital
Vision, 17 Alamy/Stephen Barnett/ImageState,
18 Dreamstime.com, 19 Ecoscene/Peter
Hulme, 20 Dreamstime.com/Pavel Gribkov,
21 courtesy of John Deere

Contents

What are rocks?

Rocks are the solid materials that make up the Earth. These solid pieces of rock are broken up over time and mix with plant and animal remains to form soil.

⬇ Beach sand is made of tiny bits of rock and shell.

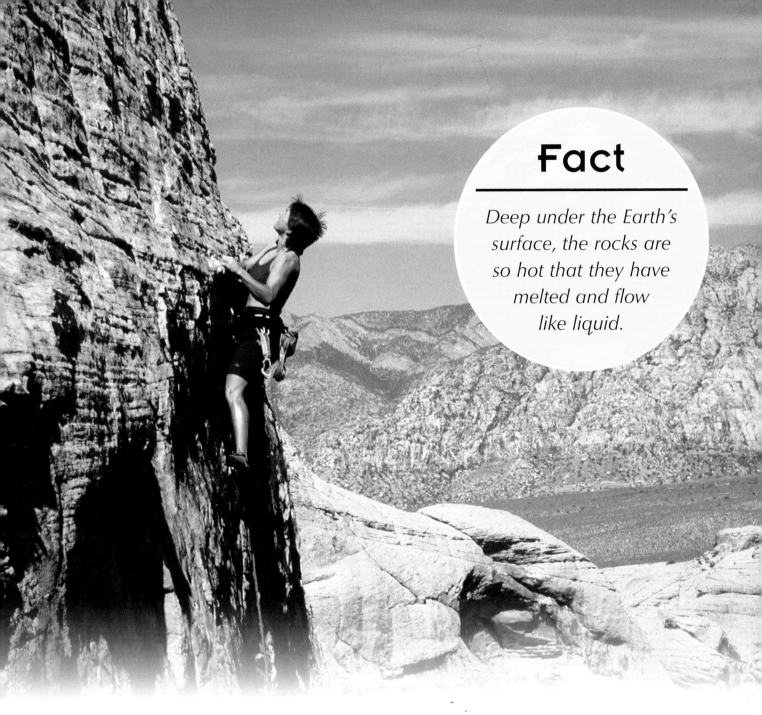

Fact

Deep under the Earth's surface, the rocks are so hot that they have melted and flow like liquid.

Rocks come in many shapes and sizes. Cliff faces and boulders are large pieces of rock. Sand and gravel are tiny pieces. Rocks may be hard, like granite, or soft, like chalk.

Mountains are made from huge pieces of rock that have been pushed high into the air.

How are rocks made?

There are three main types of rock. **Volcanic** rocks such as granite form when hot, melted rock flows out of a **volcano**, and then cools and hardens.

⊻ Liquid **lava** comes from deep under the Earth's surface.

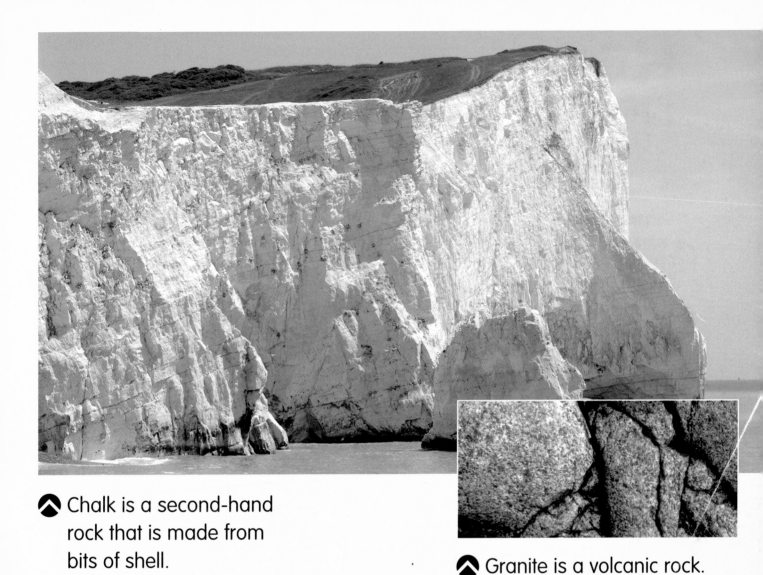

⬆ Chalk is a second-hand rock that is made from bits of shell.

⬆ Granite is a volcanic rock.

Chalk and sandstone are 'second-hand' rocks. They form when bits of rock or shell on the seabed are squashed into layers. Marble and slate are 'changed' rocks. They form when other rocks are squashed or heated deep beneath the ground.

⬆ Marble is a changed rock that is made when limestone is squashed underground.

Rocks and the weather

Wind, water and ice wear away rocks. Frost and ice can break rocks into pieces. Wind and rain can carve smooth shapes into rocks.

▼ In western USA, the Grand Canyon has been shaped by the flow of the Colorado river.

Rivers and icy **glaciers** bash and scrape against rocks on the surface. This carves large holes into the rock, which are called valleys and canyons.

Waves beating against this seashore have shaped these cliffs and rock pillars.

9

Using rocks

We dig rocks out of the ground at mines and **quarries** and use them to make things. Hard rocks, such as granite, are used to build houses or roads.

▶▶ Marble is another hard rock that is used in buildings such as the Texas Capitol.

⬇ This potter is using a spinning wheel to shape clay into a bowl.

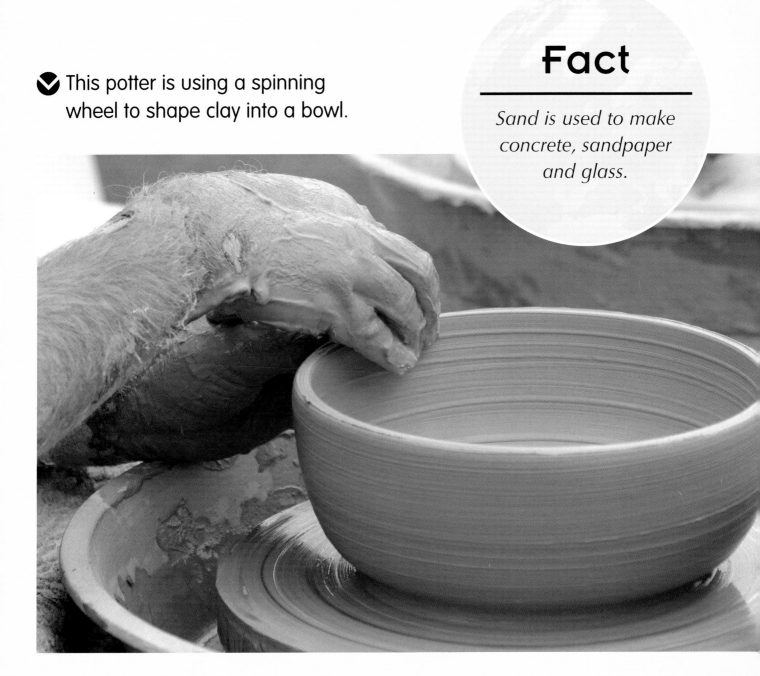

Soft rocks are also useful. Cement is made using limestone. Soft, black graphite is used to make lead for pencils. Moist, squishy clay is shaped to make bricks and pottery, and then baked in an oven to make it hard.

Metals and gems

Gold, silver and iron are **metals** found in rocks. Mixtures of rocks and metals are called **ores**. Iron ore is melted in a hot **furnace** to separate the iron from the rock.

⊗ Pieces of gold are dug out of the ground in mines or they are found in rivers.

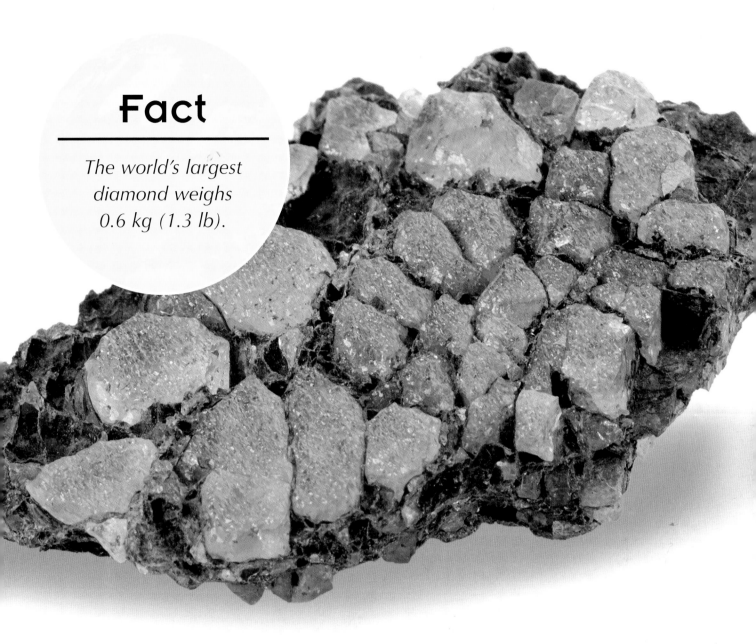

Some rocks contain **gems** such as diamonds and rubies. These gems are dug out of the ground in mines and separated from the rock. They are then cut and polished so that they sparkle.

This piece of rock contains pieces of the gem topaz. When cut and polished, topaz can be clear, yellow, brown, blue or pink.

Fossils

Fossils are the remains of animals or plants that have turned into rock. After these plants and animals died, their remains were buried by rocks and soil and slowly turned into rock over millions of years.

This is an ammonite fossil. Ammonites were shellfish that lived in the oceans millions of years ago.

Fossils remain buried until scientists dig them up. The fossils may have broken up beneath the ground. Scientists then have to put the fossil pieces together carefully to find out what the plant or animal looked like.

These scientists are removing soil to uncover the fossil of a dinosaur's leg bone.

Fossil fuels

Coal, oil and gas are called **fossil fuels**. They are the remains of plants or animals that lived millions of years ago. These remains are buried under layers of rocks and soil.

❯ Oil rigs pump oil and gas from beneath the ocean floor.

We burn fossil fuels in **power stations** to produce electricity. Cars, buses and trains run on diesel or petrol, which are made from oil.

Coal is mined using drills and special cutting machines.

17

Soil

Soil is made from tiny pieces of rock that have been broken down by the weather. Soil can be chalky, sandy or like peat, depending on the type of rock it was made from.

❯❯ Crumbly **peat** is the best type of soil to use for potted plants.

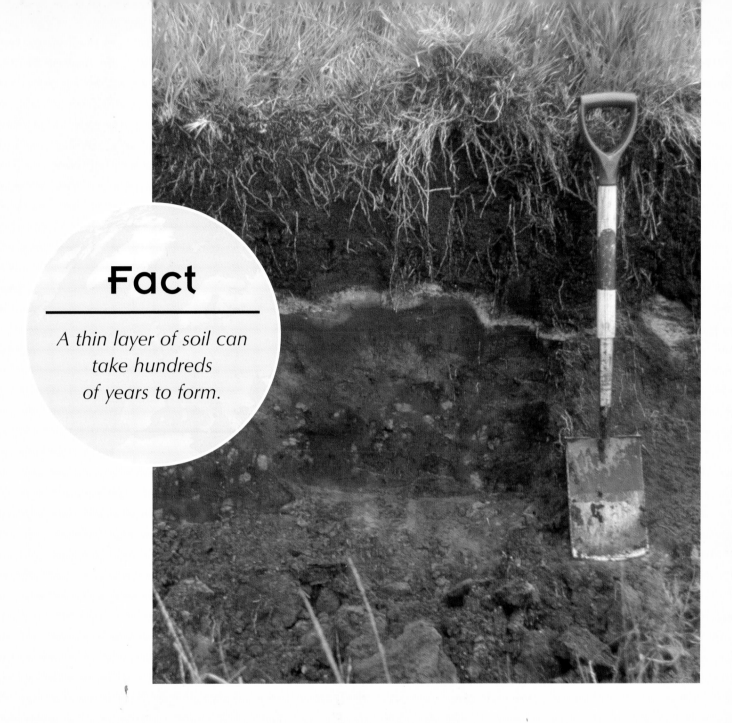

Fact
_____

A thin layer of soil can take hundreds of years to form.

Soil is formed in layers. The top layer of soil contains rich, dark **humus**, made from rotting leaves. The layers below contain larger stones, and at the bottom is solid rock.

⬆ You can see the layers of soil in this picture.

Living in the soil

Soil contains the remains of plants and animals. These add nourishing **minerals** to the soil. Plants and trees use these nourishing minerals and water.

⊗ Many small animals live in the soil, eating plants. These attract larger animals, such as moles.

Farmers grow **crops** in the soil to provide food.

Animals living in the soil include moles, rabbits and small creatures such as worms, slugs and beetles. When plants and animals die, their bodies break down, adding more minerals to the soil, so that more plants can grow.

Fact

One square metre (1.2 sq yards) of soil contains millions of living things, but most are too small to see!

Activities

Sinking in sand

Sand is made from tiny pieces of rock which make it very soft. See how far thick and thin objects sink into sand with this activity.

WHAT YOU NEED

- Bowl of sand
- Bag of sugar
- Tape measure
- Thin and thick blocks of wood
- Plank of wood

1. Place the thick block of wood onto the sand. Rest the plank of wood on top and place the bag of sugar onto the plank.

2. Leave for one minute, then remove everything and measure the depth of the mark left in the sand.

3. Repeat using the thin block. You will see that the thin block sinks deeper into the sand.

Measure the depth of each 'footprint'.

Rock freezing

Use this activity to see how the weather can break apart pieces of rock.

WHAT YOU NEED

- One rock
- Foil tray
- Jug of water
- Freezer
- Magnifying glass

1. Place the piece of rock in the tray and cover it with water from the jug.
2. Put the tray in the freezer and leave it for a day.
3. Take the tray out of the freezer and let the ice melt.
4. Pour the water out and rub your finger over the rock's surface. You might find that small pieces of grit are rubbed away. The cold from the freezer has broken up the rock's surface, making it crumble.

Glossary

Bacteria Tiny living things that are too small to see with the naked eye.

Crops Plants that are grown by farmers for food.

Fossil fuels Fuels that are made from the remains of plants or animals that lived millions of years ago.

Furnace A very hot fire that is used to melt metal.

Gems Minerals that can be cut or polished to make a jewel.

Glaciers Large bodies of ice.

Humus A layer of rich, dark material in the soil.

Lava Super-hot rock that has melted and flows out of a volcano and over the ground.

Metals Solid materials that are usually hard and shiny, such as iron and gold.

Minerals The solid substances from which rocks are made.

Ores Rocks or minerals that contain a metal.

Peat A type of soil that is very crumbly.

Power stations Places that produce electricity.

Quarries Places where rocks are dug from the ground.

Volcanic To do with volcanoes.

Volcano A weak point in Earth's crust through which lava flows when the volcano erupts.

Index